Materials

Felt

Curly Wool Yarn

Muslin & Fabric Scraps

Acrylic Paint

Chenille Stems

Fine Tip Permanent Markers

Buttons

Pin Backs

Wood Doll Parts

Sponge Brush

Embroidery Floss

Wood Button Plugs

Basic Tips

Patterns

Trace patterns and transfer to cardboard. Cut around the pattern lines carefully to make templates. Place templates on felt or fabric and trace. Using fabric scissors, cut out fabric and felt pieces

Wire

Add wire to felt pieces to allow you to shape them. Place a bead of hot glue next to one edge of felt, fold felt edge over to cover wire. Glue other edge of felt piece on top of folded edge, aligning edges evenly.

Hangers

Curl wire around a pencil. Pull wire ends to loosen and shape coils. Bend a loop in each end of wire. Hot glue loops to back of project as instructed.

Sew

Sew fabric pieces together with right sides facing, using 1/4" seams. Turn right side out. Sew felt pieces together with wrong sides facing, using 1/8" seams, unless instructed otherwise.

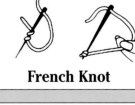

Blanket Stitch

French Knot

Running Stitch

Straight Stitch

Large Shaggy Bear

FRONT COVER PHOTO

MATERIALS:

¼ yard of Brown shaggy felt • 6" square of Brown felt • Scrap of Black felt • Brown and Black sewing threads • Two 9mm Black button eyes • Four ¾" Black buttons • 5" soft sculpture needle • 18" of Red/White ¾" ribbon • Polyester fiberfill

INSTRUCTIONS:

Felt - Fold shaggy felt in half with right sides facing. Trace pattern pieces. Cut pieces according to patterns.

Body, Arms & Legs - Sew pieces together, using ¼" seams. Leave openings as shown on patterns. Turn pieces to right side. Stuff each piece firmly and hand stitch openings closed.

Head - Sew head from A to B. Sew ears, turn, stuff and sew bottoms closed. Sew eyes, nose and ears on head. Sew head back to head, matching C's at neck and top of head. Turn head to right side. Stuff head and sew closed at neck base. Sew head to body, stitching around base 2 or 3 times to secure head in place.

Attach Arms, Legs - Align dots on arms and body to position arms. Stitch arms in place going back and forth through body and arms several times. Add buttons and repeat 2 more times. Secure thread. Use the same technique to attach legs.

Finish - Tie ribbon in a bow around neck.

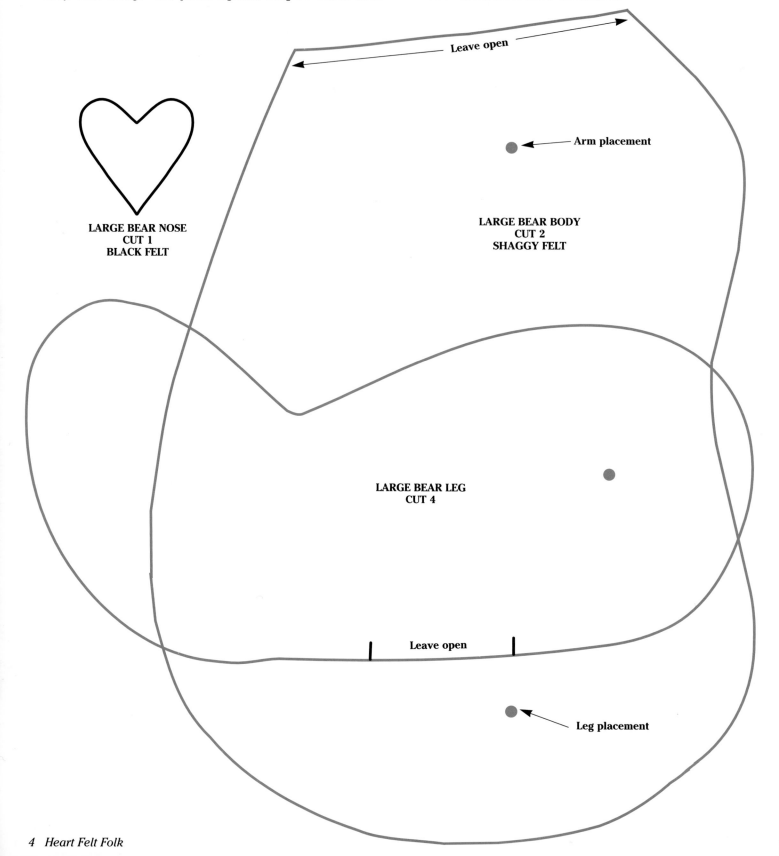

LARGE BEAR NOSE
CUT 1
BLACK FELT

LARGE BEAR BODY
CUT 2
SHAGGY FELT

Leave open

Arm placement

LARGE BEAR LEG
CUT 4

Leave open

Leg placement

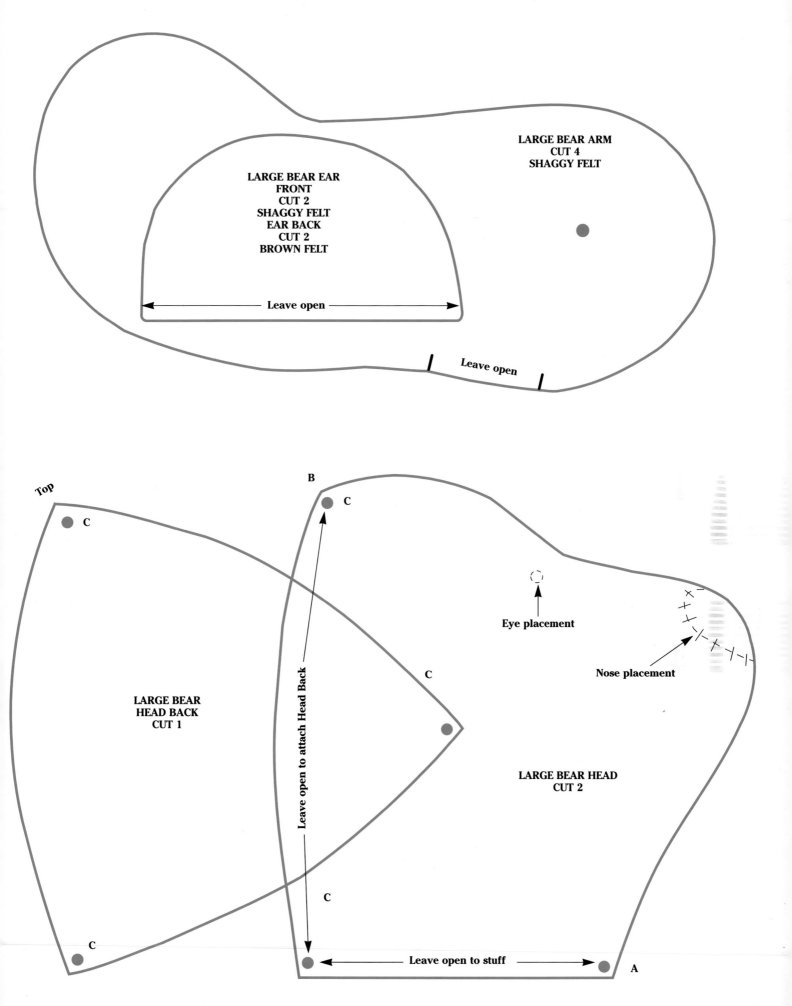

LARGE BEAR EAR
FRONT
CUT 2
SHAGGY FELT
EAR BACK
CUT 2
BROWN FELT

LARGE BEAR ARM
CUT 4
SHAGGY FELT

Leave open

Leave open

Top

B

C

C

Eye placement

Nose placement

LARGE BEAR
HEAD BACK
CUT 1

C

Leave open to attach Head Back

C

LARGE BEAR HEAD
CUT 2

C

C

Leave open to stuff

A

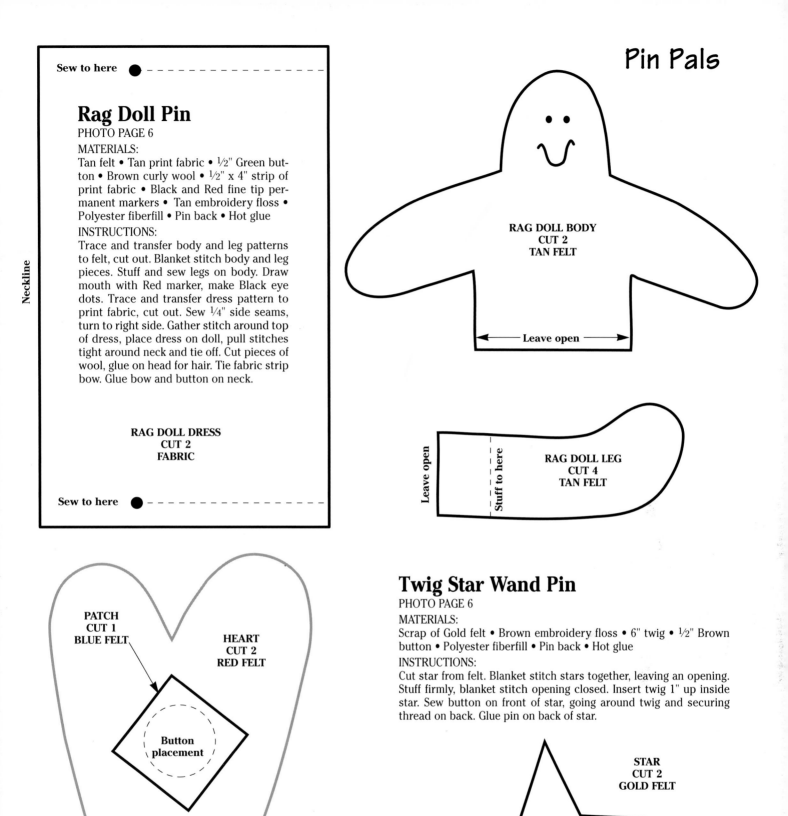

Rag Doll Pin

PHOTO PAGE 6

MATERIALS:

Tan felt • Tan print fabric • ½" Green button • Brown curly wool • ½" x 4" strip of print fabric • Black and Red fine tip permanent markers • Tan embroidery floss • Polyester fiberfill • Pin back • Hot glue

INSTRUCTIONS:

Trace and transfer body and leg patterns to felt, cut out. Blanket stitch body and leg pieces. Stuff and sew legs on body. Draw mouth with Red marker, make Black eye dots. Trace and transfer dress pattern to print fabric, cut out. Sew ¼" side seams, turn to right side. Gather stitch around top of dress, place dress on doll, pull stitches tight around neck and tie off. Cut pieces of wool, glue on head for hair. Tie fabric strip bow. Glue bow and button on neck.

Sew to here ●

Neckline

RAG DOLL DRESS
CUT 2
FABRIC

Sew to here ●

Pin Pals

RAG DOLL BODY
CUT 2
TAN FELT

Leave open

Leave open

Stuff to here

RAG DOLL LEG
CUT 4
TAN FELT

PATCH
CUT 1
BLUE FELT

HEART
CUT 2
RED FELT

Button
placement

Red Heart Pin

PHOTO PAGE 6

MATERIALS:

Red felt • 1" square of Blue felt • ¾" Tan button • Yellow embroidery floss • Polyester fiberfill • Pin back • Hot glue

INSTRUCTIONS:

Trace and transfer heart pattern to Red felt, cut out. Blanket stitch Blue patch on front of heart. Sew button in place. Blanket stitch heart pieces together, leaving an opening for stuffing. Stuff firmly, blanket stitch opening closed. Glue pin back in place.

Twig Star Wand Pin

PHOTO PAGE 6

MATERIALS:

Scrap of Gold felt • Brown embroidery floss • 6" twig • ½" Brown button • Polyester fiberfill • Pin back • Hot glue

INSTRUCTIONS:

Cut star from felt. Blanket stitch stars together, leaving an opening. Stuff firmly, blanket stitch opening closed. Insert twig 1" up inside star. Sew button on front of star, going around twig and securing thread on back. Glue pin on back of star.

STAR
CUT 2
GOLD FELT

Button
placement

More Pin Pals

Snowman Pin

PHOTO PAGE 6

MATERIALS:

Felt scraps (White, Green, Yellow, Red, Dark Blue, Orange) • ½" Gold jingle bell • ½" Blue button • White and Orange embroidery flosses • Green sewing thread • Black fine tip permanent marker • Polyester fiberfill • Pin back • Hot glue

INSTRUCTIONS:

Trace and transfer patterns to felt, cut out. Cut ¼" strip of Yellow for hatband and a ⅝" x 8" strip of Red for scarf. Layer body pieces. Sew ⅛" seam around edge leaving a 1½" opening, turn to right side and stuff firmly. Sew opening closed. Fold hat, sew running stitches down long sides. Glue hat on head and glue trim around bottom. Fold hat tip down, glue to secure. Glue bell at tip of hat. Sew nose on face with floss. Cut fringe in ends of scarf, glue around neck. Glue button on scarf. Glue heart on body as shown in photo. Glue pin in place.

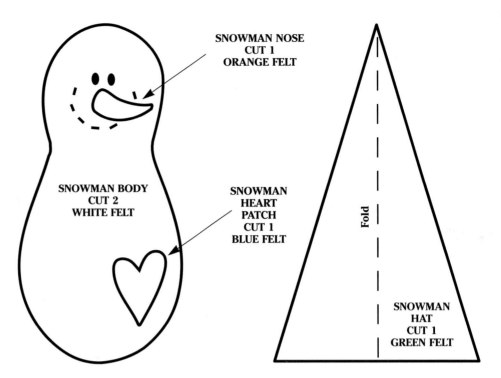

SNOWMAN NOSE CUT 1 ORANGE FELT

SNOWMAN BODY CUT 2 WHITE FELT

SNOWMAN HEART PATCH CUT 1 BLUE FELT

Fold

SNOWMAN HAT CUT 1 GREEN FELT

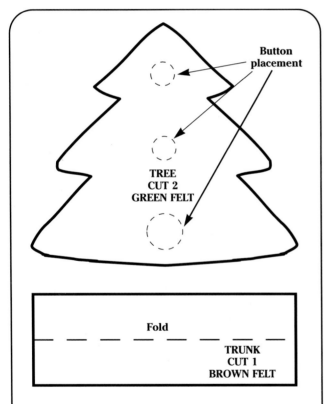

Button placement

TREE CUT 2 GREEN FELT

Fold

TRUNK CUT 1 BROWN FELT

Felt Pine Tree Pin

PHOTO PAGE 6

MATERIALS:

Scraps of Green and Brown felt • one ⅜" and two ¼" Pearl buttons • Embroidery flosses (Green, Brown, White) • Pin back • Hot glue

INSTRUCTIONS:

Trace and transfer patterns to felt, cut out. Sew buttons on front of tree with White floss. Fold trunk in half, blanket stitch around edges and stuff. Blanket stitch tree leaving small opening in center bottom. Stuff, insert trunk and stitch opening closed through all layers. Glue pin back in place.

Teddy Bear Pin

PHOTO PAGE 6

MATERIALS:

Tan felt • Brown embroidery floss • ½" x 4" strip of Red check fabric• Cosmetic blush • Black fine tip permanent marker • Polyester fiberfill • Pin back • Hot glue

INSTRUCTIONS:

Trace and transfer patterns to felt, cut out. Blanket stitch body, leaving an opening for stuffing. Stuff lightly, blanket stitch opening closed. Dot eyes and mouth with marker. Tie fabric strip bow, glue on neck. Glue pin back in place.

TEDDY BEAR CUT 2 TAN FELT

Leave open

Gold Baby Pin

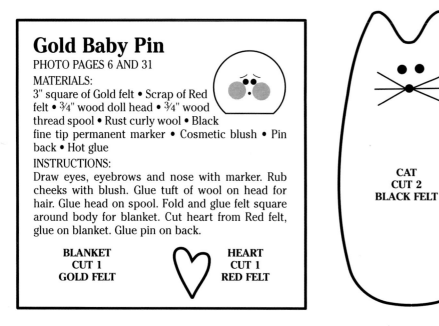

PHOTO PAGES 6 AND 31
MATERIALS:
3" square of Gold felt • Scrap of Red felt • ¾" wood doll head • ¾" wood thread spool • Rust curly wool • Black fine tip permanent marker • Cosmetic blush • Pin back • Hot glue
INSTRUCTIONS:
Draw eyes, eyebrows and nose with marker. Rub cheeks with blush. Glue tuft of wool on head for hair. Glue head on spool. Fold and glue felt square around body for blanket. Cut heart from Red felt, glue on blanket. Glue pin on back.

BLANKET
CUT 1
GOLD FELT

HEART
CUT 1
RED FELT

CAT
CUT 2
BLACK FELT

Cat Pin

PHOTO PAGE 6
MATERIALS:
Black felt • Black and Cream embroidery flosses • 26 gauge wire • Polyester fiberfill • Pin back • Hot glue
INSTRUCTIONS:
Trace and transfer body pattern to felt, cut out. Cut a ½" x 5" piece of felt for tail. Using Cream floss, make French knot eyes on body front. Blanket stitch body pieces together, leaving open at bottom. Stuff firmly, blanket stitch opening closed. Fold tail piece in half lengthwise, blanket stitch across end and half way up side. Insert wire and glue to secure. Trim wire even with end of tail. Blanket stitch remainder of tail closed. Wrap tail loosely around a pencil to form a curl. Glue tail on back of cat at one lower corner. Cut 4 strands of floss 1¼" long. Tie a knot in center of strands, glue on face for whiskers. Glue pin back in place.

Flag Pin

PHOTO PAGE 6
MATERIALS:
Felt scraps (Burgundy, Tan, Navy Blue) • Tan embroidery floss • ⅝" White square shank button • Polyester fiberfill • Pin back • Hot glue
INSTRUCTIONS:
Trace and transfer patterns to felt, cut out. Sew Tan and Navy Blue stripes on Burgundy flag front with running stitches across center of flag front. Do not sew edges of stripes in place. Blanket stitch flag front to Blue back, attaching outer edges of Blue and Tan stripes. Leave one end open. Stuff firmly, blanket stitch opening closed. Position button as shown in photo, sew through all layers to secure button in place. Glue pin on back.

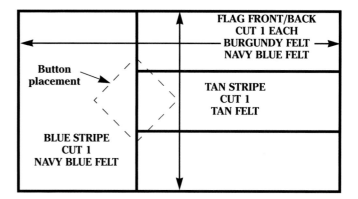

Button placement

FLAG FRONT/BACK
CUT 1 EACH
BURGUNDY FELT
NAVY BLUE FELT

TAN STRIPE
CUT 1
TAN FELT

BLUE STRIPE
CUT 1
NAVY BLUE FELT

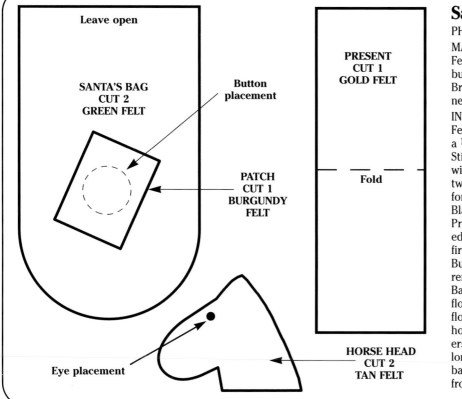

Leave open

SANTA'S BAG
CUT 2
GREEN FELT

Button placement

PATCH
CUT 1
BURGUNDY FELT

PRESENT
CUT 1
GOLD FELT

Fold

Eye placement

HORSE HEAD
CUT 2
TAN FELT

Santa's Bag Pin

PHOTO PAGE 6
MATERIALS:
Felt scraps (Green, Burgundy, Gold, Tan) • ½" Green button • Embroidery floss (Green, Tan, Gold) • Brown curly wool • 3" twig • Black fine tip permanent marker • Polyester fiberfill • Pin back • Hot glue
INSTRUCTIONS:
Felt - Trace and transfer patterns to felt, cut out. Cut a ¼" x 6" strip of Burgundy for ribbon.
Stick horse - Blanket stitch horse heads together with Tan floss, leaving bottom open. Stuff, insert twig and glue to secure. Glue loops of wool on head for mane. Draw eyes on each side of head with Black marker.
Present - Fold felt in half. Blanket stitch around edges with Gold floss, leaving one side open. Stuff firmly and blanket stitch opening closed. Glue 2" of Burgundy strip on front of present for ribbon. Using remaining strip, tie bow and glue at top of present.
Bag - Blanket stitch around edges of bag with Green floss, leaving top open. Stuff bag lightly. Using Green floss, gather stitch around top of bag. Place stick horse and present in bag, glue to secure. Pull gathers slightly, secure thread. Cut 2 strands of floss 4" long, tie strands in a bow and glue to front center of bag on gathering stitches. Glue patch and button on front of bag. Glue pin on back.

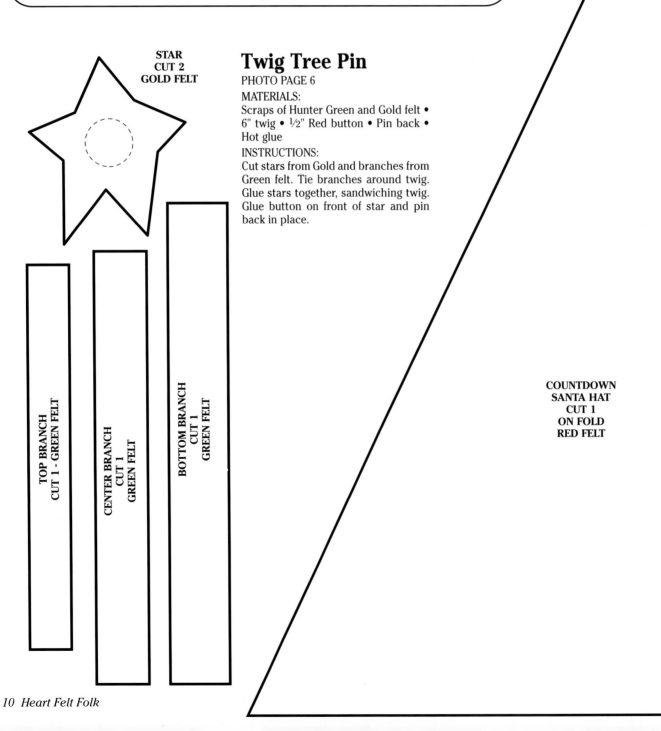

You are Loved!

'You are Loved' Block

FRONT COVER PHOTO

MATERIALS:

2¼" x 6¼" piece of ¾" wood • Antique White and Red felt • Black paint pen • 4 Black ½" buttons

INSTRUCTIONS:

Cut Ivory felt to cover top of wood piece, glue in place. Cut ⅜" strips of Red felt, glue around edge of Ivory felt, overlapping corners. Write 'You are Loved' with paint pen. Glue buttons in place at corners.

STAR
CUT 2
GOLD FELT

Twig Tree Pin

PHOTO PAGE 6

MATERIALS:

Scraps of Hunter Green and Gold felt • 6" twig • ½" Red button • Pin back • Hot glue

INSTRUCTIONS:

Cut stars from Gold and branches from Green felt. Tie branches around twig. Glue stars together, sandwiching twig. Glue button on front of star and pin back in place.

TOP BRANCH
CUT 1 - GREEN FELT

CENTER BRANCH
CUT 1
GREEN FELT

BOTTOM BRANCH
CUT 1
GREEN FELT

COUNTDOWN
SANTA HAT
CUT 1
ON FOLD
RED FELT

Place on fold

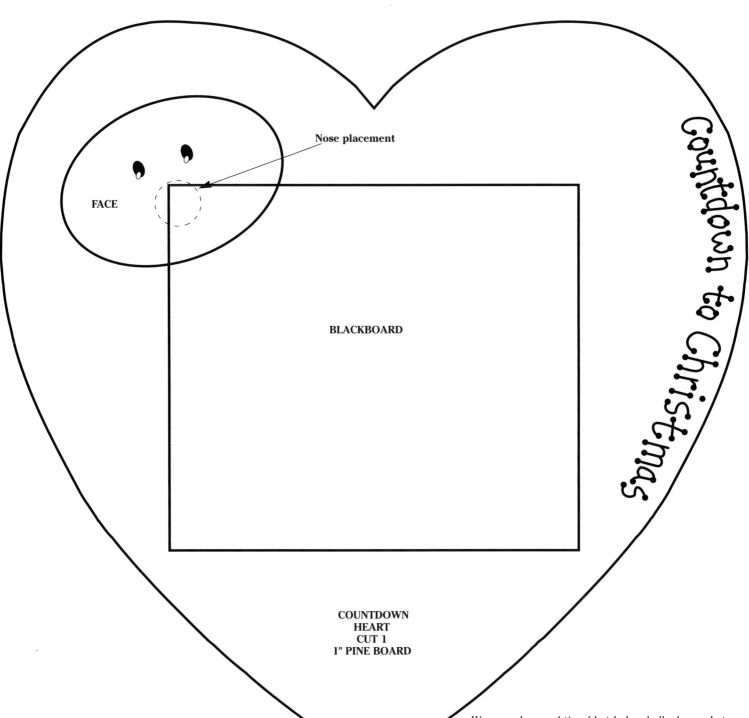

Nose placement

FACE

BLACKBOARD

COUNTDOWN
HEART
CUT 1
1" PINE BOARD

Countdown to Christmas

Countdown to Christmas Plaque

FRONT COVER PHOTO

MATERIALS:

10" square of 1" pine • Red felt square • Black, Fleshtone, White and Green acrylic paints • Paintbrush • Chalk • ¾" Gold jingle bell • ½" button plug • Cotton cord • Cotton batting • Black fine tip permanent marker • 19 and 26 gauge wire • Craft saw • Sandpaper • Hot glue

INSTRUCTIONS:

Heart - Trace patterns and make templates. Transfer heart pattern to pine, cut out and sand smooth. Paint heart Green, let dry. Sand edges. Center square template on heart as shown on pattern and trace. Paint square Black, let dry. Place a piece of chalk on its side and cover entire square. Wipe clean with a paper towel.

Hat - Cut hat from Red felt. Glue a 12½" piece of 26 gauge wire to one long side, leaving excess at bottom. Glue sides of hat together. Glue jingle bell on tip of hat. Fit hat over left half of heart, glue in place, glue end of wire to back of heart. Glue cord around bottom edge of hat.

Wrap cord around tip of hat below bell, glue ends to secure. Bend wire to shape hat.

Face - Transfer pattern to heart as shown. Glue button plug for nose. Paint face and nose Fleshtone. Paint eyes Black, add White highlights. Rub blush on cheeks and across top of nose. Glue cotton batting for beard as shown in photo, fluff gently. Roll a small piece of batting between hands to make mustache, glue under nose and curl ends. Glue 2 small tufts of batting above eyes for eyebrows.

Hanger - Cut 22" of 19 gauge wire for hanger and chalk holder. Twist wire about 7" from one end to form a loop. Curl longer end of wire loosely around a pen for hanger. Pull coils gently to form a 15" hanger. Wrap other end of wire tightly around pen and bend up to shape chalk holder with twisted loop at bottom. Glue wire to back of heart leaving chalk holder free. If desired, glue 2" pieces of cord over wire glued on back of plaque to prevent scratching walls.

Finish - Write 'Countdown to Christmas' on right side of heart with marker. Add squiggles and dots at either side of words. Draw a squiggle line around Black square. Insert chalk in chalk holder.

Small Red Bear

FRONT COVER PHOTO

MATERIALS:

2 Red felt squares • Scrap of Black felt • Brown embroidery floss • Red and Black sewing threads • Two 4mm Black bead eyes • Four ¼" White buttons • 5" soft sculpture needle • Polyester fiberfill • 17" piece of raffia

INSTRUCTIONS:

Felt - Stack felt squares and trace patterns. Cut out pieces.

Body, Arms & Legs - Place pieces together and blanket stitch around edges, using 2 strands of embroidery floss. Leave openings as shown on patterns. Stuff pieces firmly and stitch closed.

Head - Sew head from A to B. Sew back of head to head matching C's at neck and top of head. Turn right side out, sew on eyes, nose and ears. Stuff head and hand stitch closed at neck base. Sew head to body, stitching around base 2 or 3 times.

Arms, Legs - Align dots on arms and body to position arms. Stitch arms in place going back and forth through body and arms several times. Add buttons and repeat 2 more times. Secure thread. Use the same technique to attach legs.

Finish - Tie raffia in a bow around neck. Knot each end.

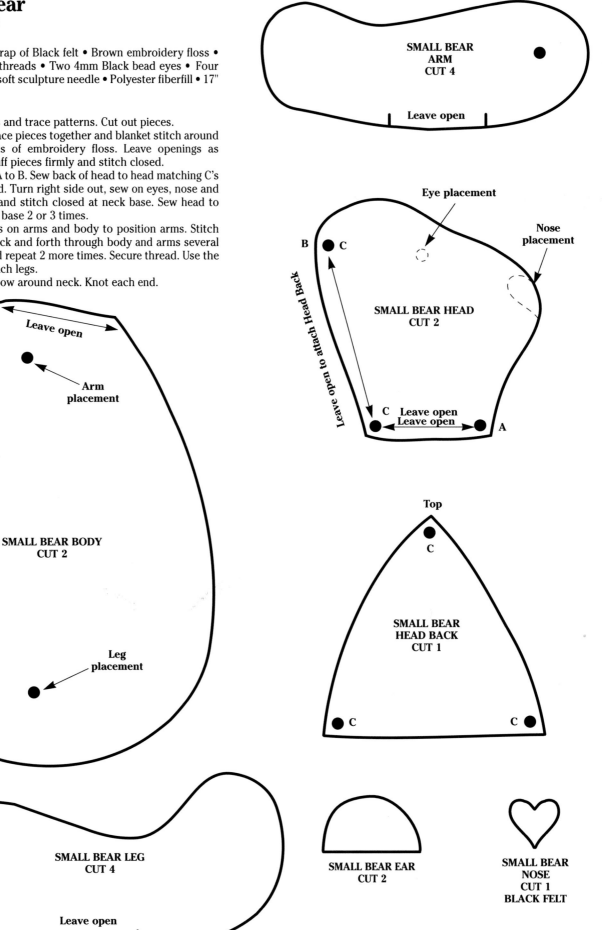

SMALL BEAR ARM CUT 4

Leave open

Eye placement

Nose placement

B C

SMALL BEAR HEAD CUT 2

Leave open to attach Head Back

C Leave open
Leave open A

Arm placement

Leave open

SMALL BEAR BODY CUT 2

Leg placement

Top

C

SMALL BEAR HEAD BACK CUT 1

C   C

SMALL BEAR LEG CUT 4

Leave open

SMALL BEAR EAR CUT 2

SMALL BEAR NOSE CUT 1 BLACK FELT

Santa Ornaments

PHOTOS ON FRONT COVER & PAGE 15

MATERIALS:

Red or Burgundy felt square • ½" x 6" strip of White felt • Red or Burgundy embroidery floss • ½" Gold jingle bell • 2 Black ½" buttons • Curly wool yarn • 1¼" wood doll head • ¼" wood button plug • Cosmetic blush • Black fine tip permanent marker • 26 gauge wire • Jute • Two 3½" twigs • Hot glue

INSTRUCTIONS:

Body - Assemble body as instructed at right. Glue felt strip down front before gathering top of body.

Head - Rub blush on cheeks, draw eyes and mouth with pen and glue button plug for nose. Glue head on top of body. Glue wool in place for beard.

Hat - Trace pattern and transfer to matching felt. Cut out hat. Glue wire to one side of hat, glue hat sides together. Glue bell on tip of hat. Glue hat on head. Twist a strand of wool to form a cord. Glue around bottom of hat. Shape hat as desired.

Trim - Glue buttons on White felt strip. Make tiny holes in sides of body, insert twig arms about 1" into body and glue to secure. Make 4" jute loop, glue on back of head.

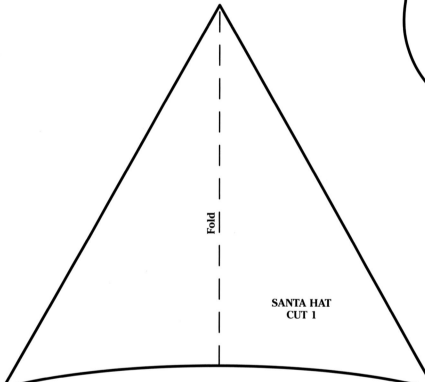

Fold

**SANTA HAT
CUT 1**

Ornaments

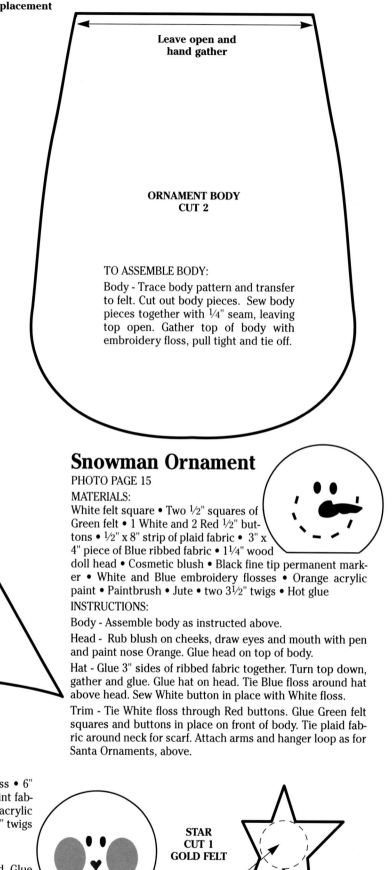

Nose
placement

Leave open and
hand gather

**ORNAMENT BODY
CUT 2**

TO ASSEMBLE BODY:

Body - Trace body pattern and transfer to felt. Cut out body pieces. Sew body pieces together with ¼" seam, leaving top open. Gather top of body with embroidery floss, pull tight and tie off.

Snowman Ornament

PHOTO PAGE 15

MATERIALS:

White felt square • Two ½" squares of Green felt • 1 White and 2 Red ½" buttons • ½" x 8" strip of plaid fabric • 3" x 4" piece of Blue ribbed fabric • 1¼" wood doll head • Cosmetic blush • Black fine tip permanent marker • White and Blue embroidery flosses • Orange acrylic paint • Paintbrush • Jute • two 3½" twigs • Hot glue

INSTRUCTIONS:

Body - Assemble body as instructed above.

Head - Rub blush on cheeks, draw eyes and mouth with pen and paint nose Orange. Glue head on top of body.

Hat - Glue 3" sides of ribbed fabric together. Turn top down, gather and glue. Glue hat on head. Tie Blue floss around hat above head. Sew White button in place with White floss.

Trim - Tie White floss through Red buttons. Glue Green felt squares and buttons in place on front of body. Tie plaid fabric around neck for scarf. Attach arms and hanger loop as for Santa Ornaments, above.

Star Lady Ornament

PHOTO PAGE 15

MATERIALS:

Burgundy felt square • Scrap of Gold felt • Burgundy embroidery floss • 6" piece of ½" Off White lace • 2 Pearl ½" buttons • 4" x ¼" piece of print fabric • Blonde doll hair • 1¼" wood doll head • Cosmetic blush • Red acrylic paint • Paintbrush • Black fine tip permanent marker • Jute • Two 3½" twigs • Hot glue

Body - Assemble body as instructed above right.

Head - Rub blush on cheeks, draw eyes with pen and paint mouth Red. Glue head on top of body. Glue hair on head.

Trim - Tie fabric bow, glue on hair. Glue lace around neck for collar. Glue a button at center of collar. Cut star from Gold felt. Glue star and remaining button in place on body front. Attach arms and hanger loop as for Santa Ornaments, above.

**STAR
CUT 1
GOLD FELT**

Button
placement

More Pin Pals

Santa Pins

PHOTOS PAGE 15

ASSEMBLY INSTRUCTIONS:

Felt - Transfer patterns to cut face, heart and 2 body pieces.

Body - Layer body pieces. Sew ¼" seam around edge leaving a 1½" opening. Stuff firmly with fiberfill and sew opening closed. Trim seam to ⅛".

Face - Glue face on body as shown on pattern. Make 2" loops of yarn, tie knot in center and glue to bottom of face for beard. Separate loops and glue to body. Glue button plug for nose. Rub blush on cheeks. Draw eyes with pen.

Trim - Glue one strand of yarn above face for hat trim. Glue bell on tip of hat. Glue heart and button in place. Glue pin in place.

Red Santa Pin

PHOTO PAGE 15

MATERIALS:

Felt scraps (Red, Gold, White) • ⅜" Gold jingle bell • White ⅜" button • White curly wool • ¼" wood button plug • Polyester fiberfill • Pin back • Hot glue

INSTRUCTIONS:

Follow Assembly Instructions, above.

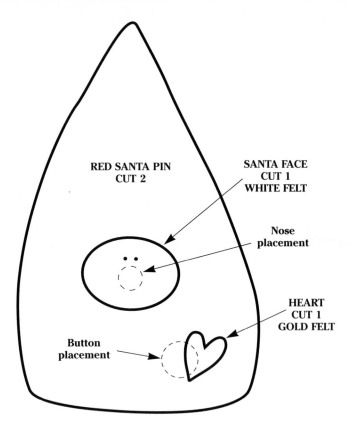

RED SANTA PIN
CUT 2

SANTA FACE
CUT 1
WHITE FELT

Nose
placement

HEART
CUT 1
GOLD FELT

Button
placement

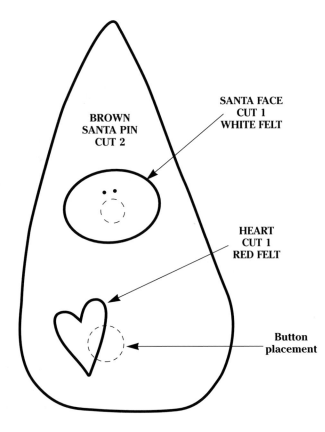

BROWN
SANTA PIN
CUT 2

SANTA FACE
CUT 1
WHITE FELT

HEART
CUT 1
RED FELT

Button
placement

Brown Santa Pin

PHOTO PAGE 15

MATERIALS:

Felt scraps (Brown, Red, White) • ⅜" Gold jingle bell • White ⅜" button • White curly wool • ¼" wood button plug • Polyester fiberfill • Pin back • Hot glue

INSTRUCTIONS:

Follow Assembly Instructions, above.

Blue Santa Pin

PHOTO PAGE 15

MATERIALS:

Felt scraps (Navy Blue, Red, White) • ⅜" Gold jingle bell • White ⅜" button • White curly wool • ¼" wood button plug • Polyester fiberfill • Pin back • Hot glue

INSTRUCTIONS:

Follow Assembly Instructions, at left.

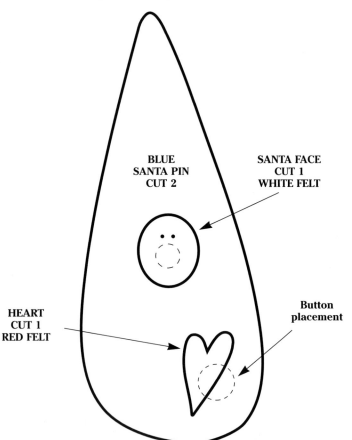

BLUE
SANTA PIN
CUT 2

SANTA FACE
CUT 1
WHITE FELT

HEART
CUT 1
RED FELT

Button
placement

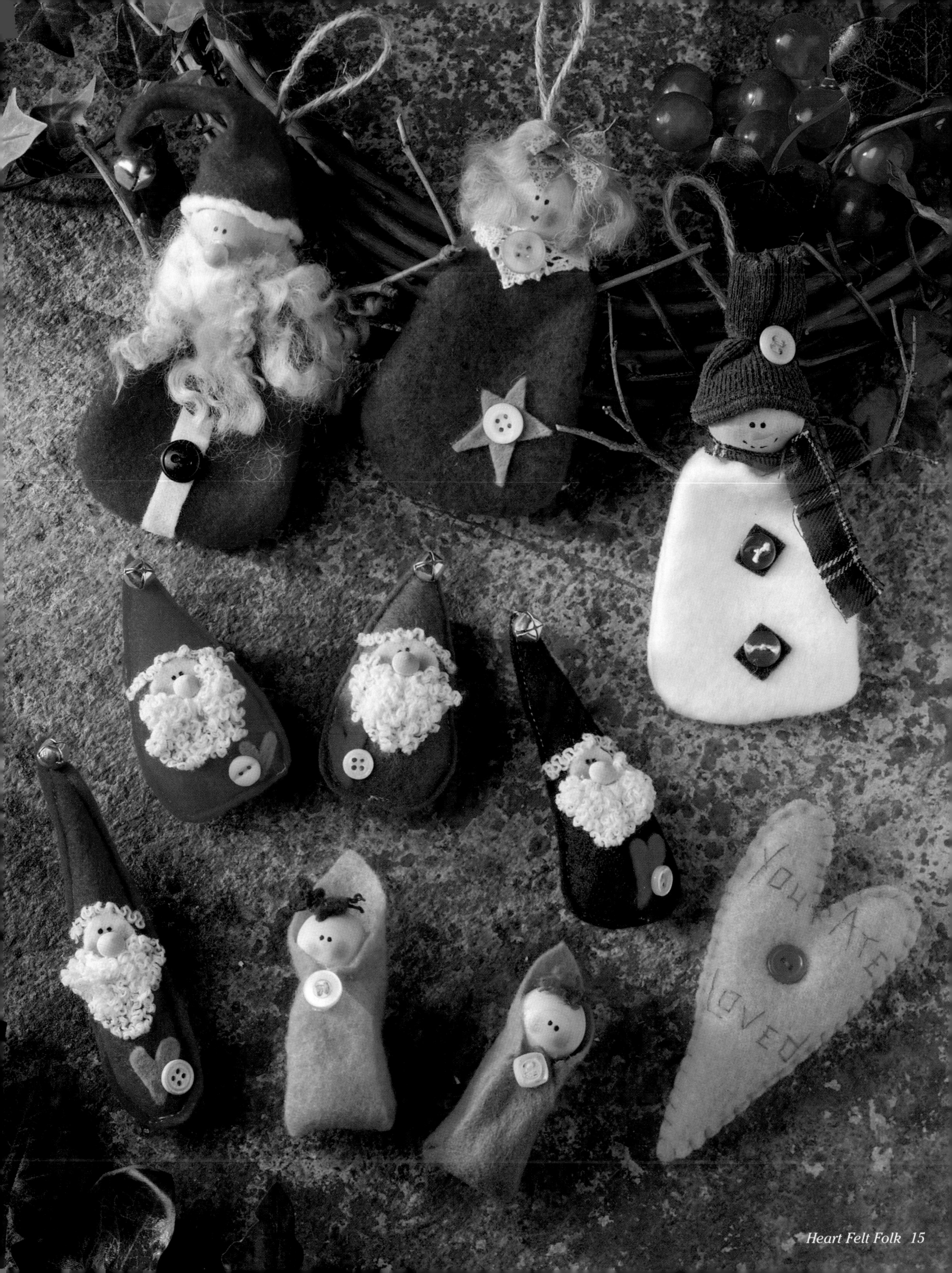
You Are Loved

Shelf Sitter Dolls

Wood Shelf Sitters

GENERAL MATERIALS:
Felt squares • 2" x 4" wood scrap • 1" pine scraps • 1/8" drill • 1 1/2" wood doll heads • Two 6" chenille stems • 26 gauge wire • Black and Red fine tip permanent markers • Buttons • Embroidery floss • Curly wool • Cosmetic blush • Black acrylic paint • Small sponge brush • Hot glue

ASSEMBLY INSTRUCTIONS:
Trace patterns.

Wood Body - Transfer wood body pattern to 2" x 4" wood piece. Cut out and drill holes in front of body for chenille stem legs.

Wood Boots - Transfer wood boot pattern to 1" pine, cut out. Paint boots Black. Drill hole in top of boot 1/8" deep. Glue half of a chenille stem in each boot.

Faces - Draw eyes and nose on wood head with Black marker. Draw mouths with Red marker. Rub blush on cheeks. Cut pieces of curly wool yarn for hair, glue on top of head. Glue head on body.

Jacket/Dress - Transfer pattern to felt and cut out. Sew 1/8" side seams to marks, turn right side out. Add embellishments according to instructions. Sew running stitches around top of dress. Place dress on doll, pull stitches tight around neck and tie off.

Arms - Transfer arm pattern to same color of felt as jacket/dress, cut out. Fold arm piece in half and sew 1/4" seam to form a tube, trim seam to 1/8". Turn to right side. Tie a knot in center of tube and glue ends to centers of slanted shoulders at sides of body.

Legs - Transfer leg pattern to color of felt indicated in project instructions, cut out. Fold leg pieces in half, sew 1/4" seam to form a tube, trim seam to 1/8". Turn to right side. Slip felt over chenille stems, glue chenille stems and legs in holes at tops of boots. Glue other end of chenille stems and legs in holes at bottom of body. Felt pieces will be longer than chenille stems and will gather slightly.

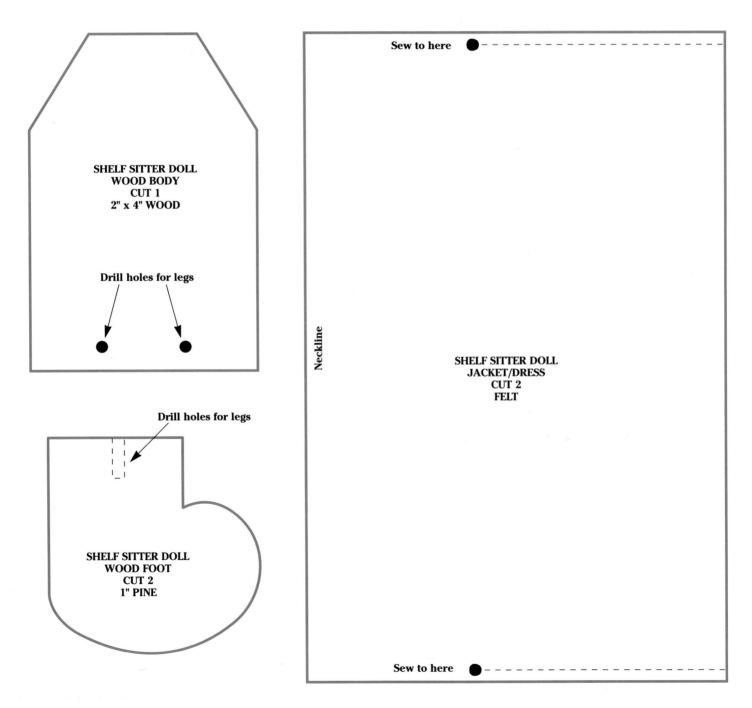

SHELF SITTER DOLL
WOOD BODY
CUT 1
2" x 4" WOOD

Drill holes for legs

Drill holes for legs

SHELF SITTER DOLL
WOOD FOOT
CUT 2
1" PINE

Sew to here

Neckline

SHELF SITTER DOLL
JACKET/DRESS
CUT 2
FELT

Sew to here

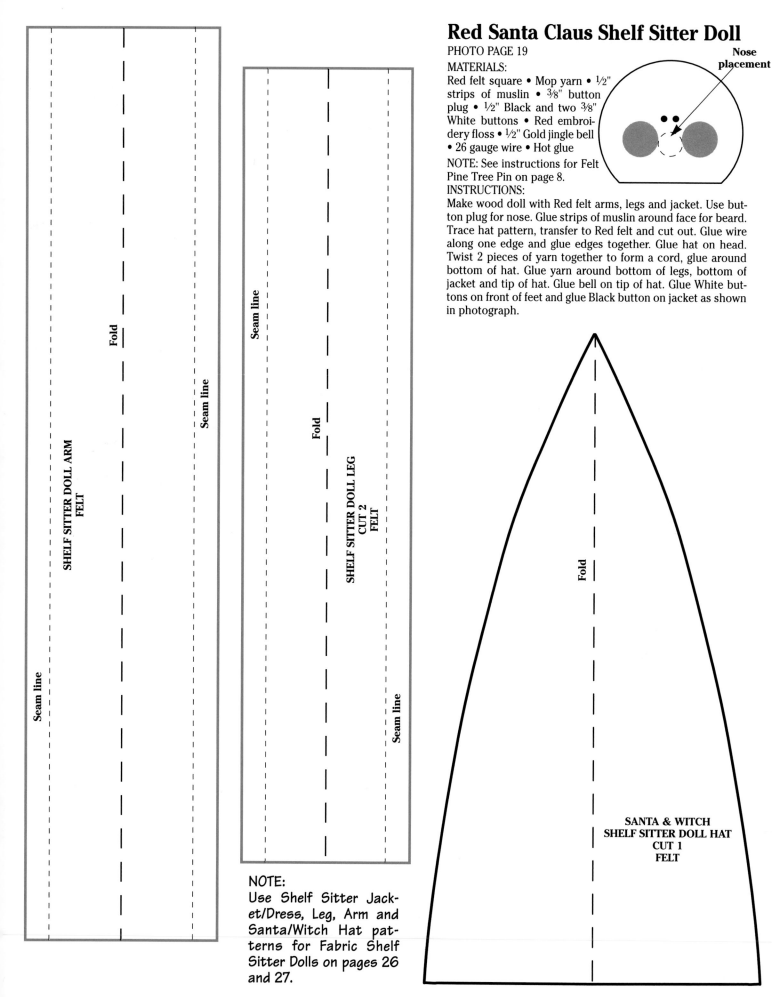

SHELF SITTER DOLL ARM
FELT

Seam line

Fold

Seam line

Seam line

SHELF SITTER DOLL LEG
CUT 2
FELT

Seam line

Fold

Seam line

NOTE:
Use Shelf Sitter Jacket/Dress, Leg, Arm and Santa/Witch Hat patterns for Fabric Shelf Sitter Dolls on pages 26 and 27.

Red Santa Claus Shelf Sitter Doll

PHOTO PAGE 19

Nose placement

MATERIALS:
Red felt square • Mop yarn • ½" strips of muslin • ⅜" button plug • ½" Black and two ⅜" White buttons • Red embroidery floss • ½" Gold jingle bell • 26 gauge wire • Hot glue

NOTE: See instructions for Felt Pine Tree Pin on page 8.

INSTRUCTIONS:
Make wood doll with Red felt arms, legs and jacket. Use button plug for nose. Glue strips of muslin around face for beard. Trace hat pattern, transfer to Red felt and cut out. Glue wire along one edge and glue edges together. Glue hat on head. Twist 2 pieces of yarn together to form a cord, glue around bottom of hat. Glue yarn around bottom of legs, bottom of jacket and tip of hat. Glue bell on tip of hat. Glue White buttons on front of feet and glue Black button on jacket as shown in photograph.

Fold

SANTA & WITCH
SHELF SITTER DOLL HAT
CUT 1
FELT

See instructions for Fabric Shelf Sitter Dolls on pages 26 and 27.

Whimsical Dolls, Santas, Bunnies, and Bears will warm your heart throughout the year!

See instructions for Wood Shelf Sitter Dolls on pages 16 and 17 and on pages 20 and 21.

More Wood Shelf Sitter Dolls

Uncle Sam Shelf Sitter Doll

PHOTO PAGE 18

MATERIALS:
Navt Blue and Tan felt squares • Burgundy felt scrap • Blue and White embroidery floss • ½" x 8" strip of Tan print fabric • ¼" button plug • White curly wool • Two ⅝" Burgundy buttons and one ¼" White button • Hot glue

NOTE: See instructions for Flag Pin on page 9.

INSTRUCTIONS:
Trace patterns for wood body and feet as well as felt legs, arms and jacket on pages 16 and 17. Make wood doll with Dark Blue felt arms and jacket, Tan felt legs. Glue button plug in place for nose and wool loops for beard. Transfer stovepipe hat brim/top to Dark Blue felt, cut out. Cut a 4½" x 2" piece of Dark Blue felt for hat crown. Cut a 5¼" x ⅜" strip of Burgundy for hatband, cut a notch in one end. Glue hat crown in a cylinder. Sew brim on bottom and glue circle on top. Begin at center front to glue hatband in place. Sew button on hatband with White floss. Cut fabric strip in half. Knot a piece around the bottom of each leg. Glue Burgundy buttons to front of wood feet.

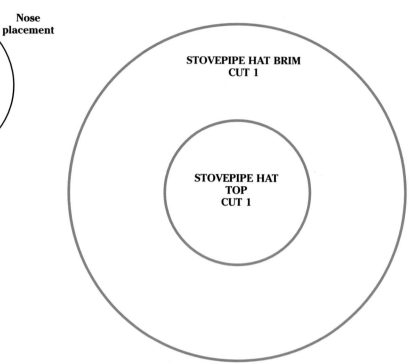

Nose placement

STOVEPIPE HAT BRIM
CUT 1

STOVEPIPE HAT TOP
CUT 1

Girl Shelf Sitter Doll with Dark Blue Dress

PHOTO PAGE 19

MATERIALS:
Denim and Tan felt squares • 1" square of Red felt • ½" x 18" strip of Red print fabric • Rust curly wool • One ¼" White and one ⅝" Red button • Blue embroidery floss • Hot glue

NOTE: See instructions for Teddy Bear Pin on page 8.

INSTRUCTIONS:
Trace patterns for wood body and foot as well as felt legs, arms and jacket on pages 16 and 17. Make wood doll with Denim felt arms and jacket, Tan legs. Glue Red felt square, a ½" fabric patch and small button on dress as shown in photo. Cut two 3" pieces of fabric strip. Tie one piece around top of each leg. Tie remaining strip in a bow. Glue bow on head behind hair and glue Red button at neck.

Bunny Shelf Sitter Doll

PHOTO PAGES 18 & 19

MATERIALS:
Dark Cranberry felt square • Felt scraps (Tan, Antique Gold, Green, Dark Brown) • ½" x 18" strip of print fabric • Pink paint pen • ½" Gold button • Red embroidery floss

NOTE: See instructions for Twig Tree Pin on page 10.

INSTRUCTIONS:
Trace patterns for wood body and feet as well as felt legs, arms and jacket on pages 16 and 17. Make wood doll with Cranberry felt arms, legs and jacket. Trace ear and flower patterns. Cut ears from Tan felt. Cut flowers from Gold, centers from Brown and leaves from Green felt. Cut a ¼" wide strip of Green felt for stems. Cut one stem 1½" long and two 2½" long. Paint Pink nose, paint whiskers, eyes and mouth Black. Rub blush down center of ears, knot ears in center and glue knot on head. Glue stems, flowers flower centers and leaves on dress as shown in photo. Cut fabric strip in thirds and tie a bow around bottom of each leg. Tie bow with remaining fabric, glue on head in front of ear knot. Glue button at neck.

BUNNY EARS
CUT 1
ON FOLD
TAN FELT

Fold

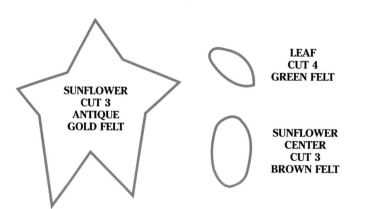

SUNFLOWER
CUT 3
ANTIQUE GOLD FELT

LEAF
CUT 4
GREEN FELT

SUNFLOWER CENTER
CUT 3
BROWN FELT

Snowman Shelf Sitter Doll

PHOTO PAGE 22

MATERIALS:
Royal Blue and Red felt squares • Felt scraps (Orange, Green, Black, Burgundy, Gold) • 3" x 6" piece of White ribbed fabric • ¼" and ½" White buttons • Embroidery floss (Blue, White, Orange, Red) • White acrylic paint • Artificial snow • Hot glue

NOTE: See instructions for Snowman Pin on page 8.

INSTRUCTIONS:
Trace patterns for wood body and feet as well as felt legs, arms and jacket on pages 16 and 17. Make wood doll with Blue felt arms and jacket, Red felt legs. Transfer stovepipe hat brim/top to Black felt according to pattern at left. Cut a 4½" x 2" piece of Black felt for hat crown. Cut a 5 x ½" strip of Gold felt for hatband, Cut Orange nose, Red heart and Green patch. Cut a ½" x 8" strip of Burgundy for scarf. Cut fringe in end of scarf. Paint head White. Sew Green patch on jacket. Sew heart and small button on patch. Fold and sew nose in carrot shape with Orange floss, pull floss slightly to make nose crooked. Glue nose on face. Glue hat crown in a cylinder. Sew brim on bottom and glue circle on top. Glue hatband in place and hat on head. Wrap and glue scarf around neck, sew large button on scarf. Cut ribbed fabric in half for socks. Fold each piece in half and sew around bottom of legs using White floss. Add snow to tip of nose and brim and top of hat.

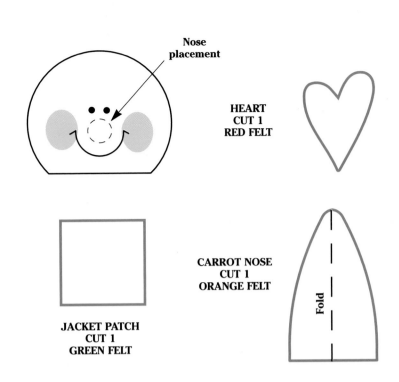

Nose placement

HEART
CUT 1
RED FELT

JACKET PATCH
CUT 1
GREEN FELT

CARROT NOSE
CUT 1
ORANGE FELT

Fold

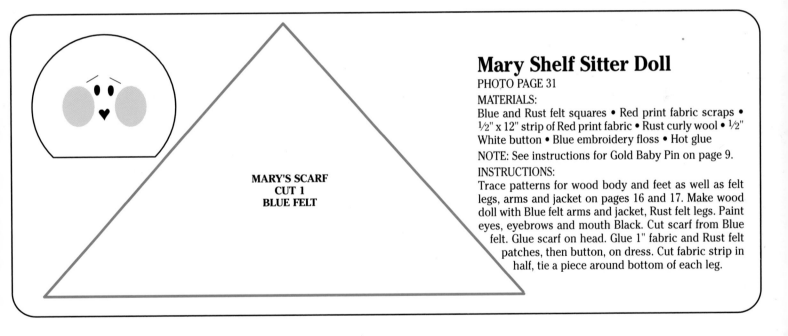

MARY'S SCARF
CUT 1
BLUE FELT

Mary Shelf Sitter Doll

PHOTO PAGE 31

MATERIALS:
Blue and Rust felt squares • Red print fabric scraps • ½" x 12" strip of Red print fabric • Rust curly wool • ½" White button • Blue embroidery floss • Hot glue

NOTE: See instructions for Gold Baby Pin on page 9.

INSTRUCTIONS:
Trace patterns for wood body and feet as well as felt legs, arms and jacket on pages 16 and 17. Make wood doll with Blue felt arms and jacket, Rust felt legs. Paint eyes, eyebrows and mouth Black. Cut scarf from Blue felt. Glue scarf on head. Glue 1" fabric and Rust felt patches, then button, on dress. Cut fabric strip in half, tie a piece around bottom of each leg.

Joseph Shelf Sitter Doll

PHOTO PAGE 31

MATERIALS:
Dark Brown and Rust felt squares • 1" x ¾" piece of Tan felt • ½" x 9" strip of Tan/Blue print fabric • Rust curly wool • ½" Blue button • Brown embroidery floss • Hot glue

NOTE: See instructions for Twig Star Wand Pin on page 7.

INSTRUCTIONS:
Trace patterns for wood body and feet as well as felt legs, arms and jacket on pages 16 and 17. Make wood doll with Brown felt arms and jacket, Rust felt legs. Cut scarf from Brown felt. Glue scarf on head. Fold pleats in scarf back and glue at center underneath scarf. Glue Tan felt patch, a fabric patch and button on dress as shown in photo. Cut remaining fabric strip in half, knot a piece around bottom of each leg.

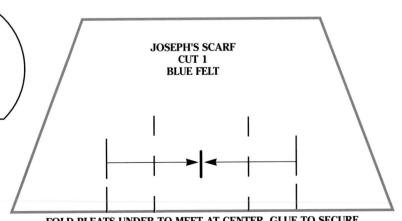

JOSEPH'S SCARF
CUT 1
BLUE FELT

FOLD PLEATS UNDER TO MEET AT CENTER, GLUE TO SECURE

Maroon Santa Pin

PHOTO PAGE 15

MATERIALS:
Felt scraps (Maroon, Gold, White) • 3/8" Gold jingle bell • White 3/8" button • White curly wool • 1/4" wood button plug • Polyester fiberfill • Pin back • Hot glue

ASSEMBLY INSTRUCTIONS:
Felt - Transfer patterns to cut face, heart and 2 body pieces.
Body - Layer body pieces. Sew 1/4" seam around edge leaving a 1 1/2" opening. Stuff firmly with fiberfill and sew opening closed. Trim seam to 1/8".
Face - Glue face on body as shown on pattern. Make 2" loops of yarn, tie knot in center and glue to bottom of face for beard. Separate loops and glue to body. Glue button plug for nose. Rub blush on cheeks. Draw eyes with pen.
Trim - Glue one strand of yarn above face for hat trim. Glue bell on tip of hat. Glue heart and button in place. Glue pin in place.

More Pin Pals

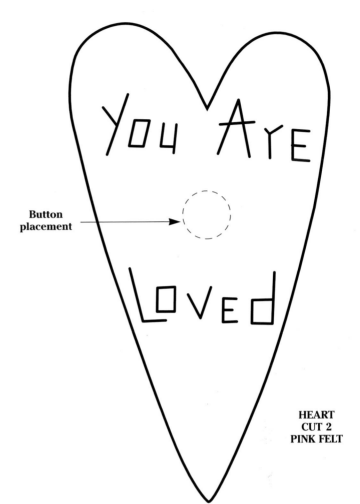

Button placement

**HEART
CUT 2
PINK FELT**

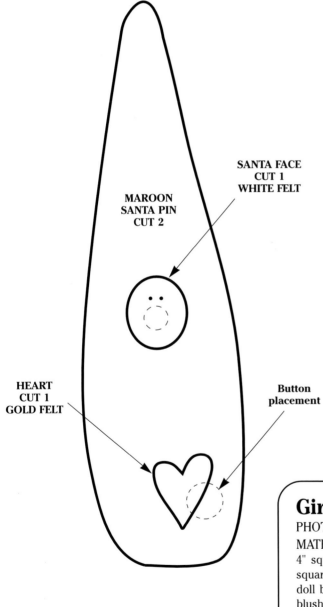

**MAROON
SANTA PIN
CUT 2**

**SANTA FACE
CUT 1
WHITE FELT**

**HEART
CUT 1
GOLD FELT**

**Button
placement**

Pink Heart Pin

PHOTO PAGE 15

MATERIALS:
Strawberry Pink felt • 1/2" Red button • Red embroidery floss • Polyester fiberfill • Pin back • Hot glue

INSTRUCTIONS:
Trace and transfer heart pattern to felt, cut out. Embroider 'You Are Loved' on front of heart. Blanket stitch heart pieces together, leaving an opening for stuffing. Stuff firmly, blanket stitch opening closed. Sew button in place at center of heart through all layers. Glue pin back in place.

Girl and Boy Baby Pins

PHOTO PAGE 15

MATERIALS:
4" squares of Pink and Blue felt • Rust curly wool • 1/4" square and 1/2" round White buttons • Two 2 1/2" wood doll bodies • Black fine tip permanent marker • Cosmetic blush • Pin backs • Hot glue

INSTRUCTIONS:
Draw eyes with Black marker. Rub cheeks with blush. Glue tufts of wool on heads for hair. Fold and glue felt squares around bodies for blankets. Glue buttons in place as shown in photo. Glue pin backs in place.

Medium Rust Bear

PHOTO PAGE 22

MATERIALS:

¼ yard of Rust classic felt • Black and Red felt scraps • Rust and Red sewing threads • Two 7mm Black button eyes • Four ¾" Black buttons • 12" of 1" Red/White torn fabric strip • 5" soft sculpture needle • Polyester fiberfill

NOTE: See instructions for Red Heart Pin on page 7.

INSTRUCTIONS:

Felt - Fold felt in half with right sides together. Trace pattern pieces on felt. Cut out pieces.

Body, Arms & Legs - Sew pieces together, using ⅛" seams. Leave openings as shown on patterns. Sew heart on chest. Turn pieces right side out, stuff firmly and hand stitch openings closed.

Head - Sew head from A to B. Sew head back to head, matching C's at neck and top of head. Turn to right side, sew on eyes, nose and ears. Stuff head and hand stitch closed at neck base. Sew head to body, stitching around base 2 or 3 times.

·Arms, Legs - Align dots on arms and body to position arms. Stitch arms in place going back and forth through body and arms several times. Add buttons and repeat 2 more times. Secure thread. Use the same technique to attach legs.

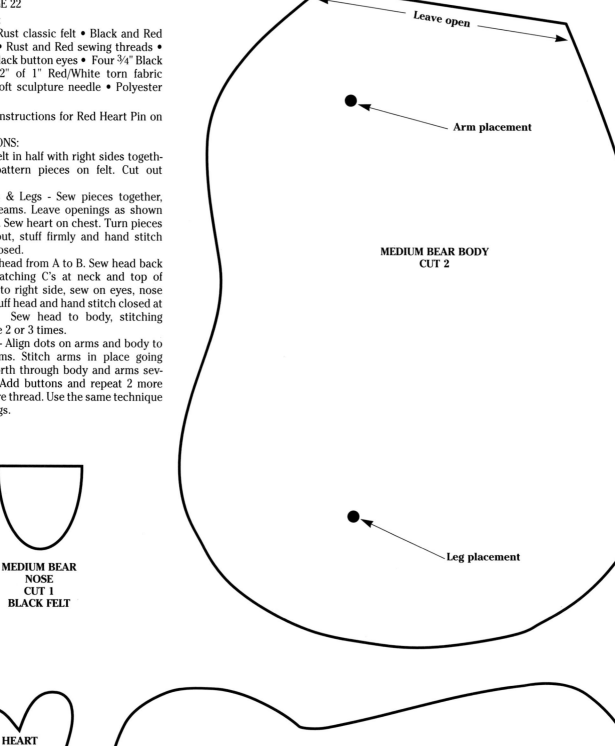

Leave open

Arm placement

MEDIUM BEAR BODY
CUT 2

Leg placement

MEDIUM BEAR
NOSE
CUT 1
BLACK FELT

HEART
PATCH
CUT 1
RED FELT

MEDIUM BEAR ARM
CUT 4

Leave open

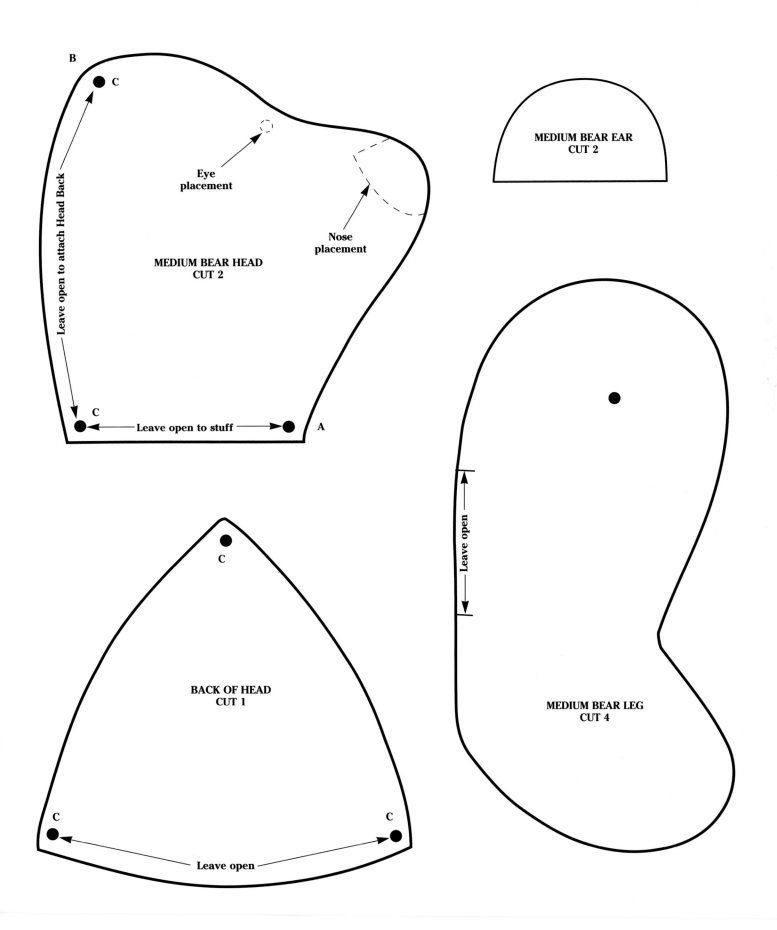

B

C

Eye
placement

Nose
placement

Leave open to attach Head Back

MEDIUM BEAR HEAD
CUT 2

C

← Leave open to stuff →

A

MEDIUM BEAR EAR
CUT 2

C

BACK OF HEAD
CUT 1

C

C

Leave open

Leave open

MEDIUM BEAR LEG
CUT 4

More Shelf Sitter Dolls

Fabric Shelf Sitter Dolls

GENERAL MATERIALS:

Muslin • 1½" wood doll heads • Two 6" chenille stems • 26 gauge wire • Ecru sewing thread• Embroidery flosses • Black and Red fine tip permanent markers • Buttons • Curly wool • Small funnel • Polyester fiberfill • Rice • Hot glue

ASSEMBLY INSTRUCTIONS:

Trace patterns.

Fabric Body - Transfer fabric body pattern to muslin and cut out. Sew ¼" seam around body, cut slit in back and turn to right side. Turn bottom corners down in a V and tack in place on bottom seam to make bottom of body square. Using a funnel, fill bottom 2" of body with rice then stuff top of body firmly with fiberfill. Sew slit closed.

Fabric Boots - Transfer fabric boot pattern to felt, cut out. Sew around edges, leaving top open. Turn to right side and lightly stuff toe area up to ankle. Insert one end of a chenille stem in each boot, glue to secure.

Faces - Draw eyes and nose on head with Black marker. Draw mouths with Red marker. Rub blush on cheeks. Cut pieces of curly wool yarn for hair, glue on top of head. Glue head on body.

Jacket/Dress - Transfer pattern on page 16 to felt and cut out. Sew ⅛" side seams to marks, turn to right side. Add embellishments according to instructions. Sew running stitch around top of dress. Place dress on doll, pull stitches tight around neck and tie off.

Arms - Transfer arm pattern on page 17 to same color of felt as jacket/dress, cut out. Fold arm piece in half and sew seam to form a tube, turn to right side. Tie a knot in center of tube and glue ends to shoulders.

Legs - Transfer leg pattern on page 17 to color of felt indicated in project instructions, cut out. Fold leg pieces in half, sew seam to form a tube. Turn to right side. Slip felt tube over chenille stems, glue to tops of boots. Glue chenille stems and legs on body. The felt pieces will be longer than the chenille stems and will gather slightly.

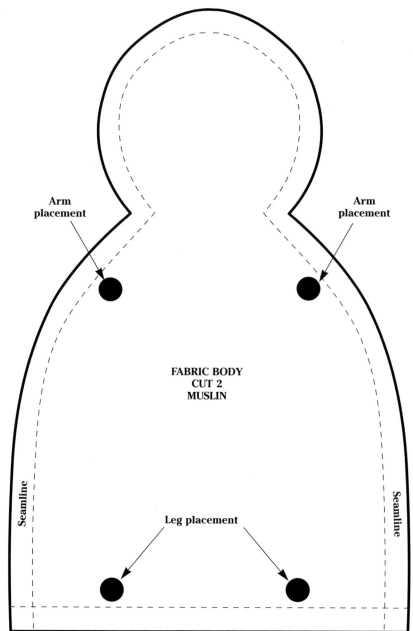

Arm placement

Arm placement

**FABRIC BODY
CUT 2
MUSLIN**

Seamline

Seamline

Leg placement

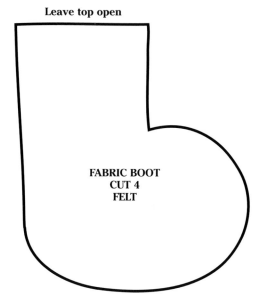

Leave top open

**FABRIC BOOT
CUT 4
FELT**

Girl Shelf Sitter Doll with Blue Dress

PHOTO PAGES 18 & 19

MATERIALS:

Cadet Blue and Burgundy felt squares • Scrap of Dark Brown felt • ½" x 18" strip of Burgundy print fabric • 1" x 10" strip of Burgundy/Gold print fabric • Two 1" squares of print fabric • Rust curly wool • ½" and ⅝" Black buttons • Blue embroidery floss • ¾" x 8" strip of print fabric • Pink paint pen • Hot glue

NOTE: See instructions for Rag Doll Pin on page 7.

INSTRUCTIONS:

Make fabric doll with Cadet Blue felt jacket and arms, Burgundy legs and Dark Brown boots. Glue fabric patches and large button on dress. Draw mouth with paint pen. Tie bow with ¾" fabric strip, glue on head. Cut two 4" pieces of ½" fabric strip. Tie one piece around top of each leg. Tie remaining strip in a bow. Glue bow and small button on neck. Tie 1" fabric strip into a bow, glue on top of hair.

Cranberry Santa Claus Shelf Sitter

PHOTO PAGES 18

MATERIALS:
Cranberry and Ivory felt squares • Scraps of Green and Gold felt• ½" strips of muslin • ⅜" button plug • ¼" and ½" White buttons • Burgundy and Ivory embroidery flosses • ½" Gold jingle bell • 26 gauge wire • Hot glue

NOTE: See instructions for Santa's Bag Pin on page 9.

INSTRUCTIONS:
Make fabric doll with Cranberry felt jacket, arms and legs. Use button plug for nose. Glue strips of muslin around face for beard. Trace and transfer Santa/Witch Hat pattern on page 17 onto Cranberry felt, cut out. Glue wire on one edge of hat and glue edges together. Glue hat on head. Cut ⅜" strips of Ivory felt, glue around bottom and tip of hat. Glue bell at tip of hat. Cut a ½" strip of Ivory felt, sew around bottom of jacket with Ivory floss and cut fringe. Using 6" of felt, tie a bow around bottom of each leg. Trace and transfer star pattern onto Gold felt, cut out. Cut patch from Green felt. Glue patch, star and buttons in place on jacket as shown in photo.

SANTA STAR
PATCH
CUT 1
GOLD FELT

SANTA
JACKET
PATCH
CUT 1
GREEN FELT

Witch Shelf Sitter Doll

PHOTO PAGES 18

MATERIALS:
Felt squares (Black, Persimmon, Dark Brown) • Scrap of Grey felt • Black curly wool • ¾" x 18" strip of Orange print fabric • ½" Orange and Black buttons • Red fine tip permanent marker • Orange and Grey embroidery flosses • 26 gauge wire • Hot glue

NOTE: See instructions for Cat Pin on page 9.

INSTRUCTIONS:
Make fabric doll with Persimmon felt jacket and arms, Dark Brown legs and Black boots. Glue 1" square Black patch and Orange button on dress. Draw mouth with Red marker. Trace hat and mouse patterns. Trace and transfer Santa/Witch Hat pattern on page 17 onto Black felt, cut out. Trace and transfer Stovepipe Hat Brim pattern on page 20 onto Black felt, cut out. Cut a 1" square from center circle. Glue wire on one edge of hat and glue edges together. Glue brim and hat on head. Using 6" of fabric strip, tie a bow around bottom of each leg. Tie bow with remaining fabric strip. Glue bow and Black button at neck. Glue 1" Black patch and Orange button on dress as shown in photo.

Mouse - Trace and transfer mouse patterns to Grey felt, cut out. Glue wire down center of tail. Blanket stitch mouse tail and body pieces together. Sew tail on body. Make whiskers with Grey floss and eyes with Black marker. Curl tail loosely around a pencil. Sew tail to tip of hat.

MOUSE BODY
CUT 2
GREY FELT

MOUSE TAIL - CUT 1 - GREY FELT

Fold

Paperweights

PAPERWEIGHT
TOP/BOTTOM
CUT 2
FELT

GIFT
TAG
CUT 1
TAN
FELT

Present Paperweight

PHOTO PAGE 35

MATERIALS:
1 square of Blue felt • 1 square of Red felt • Tan felt scrap • Blue and Red embroidery floss • Small Brass pin • Small funnel• Rice • Polyester fiberfill • Black paint pen • Hot glue

INSTRUCTIONS:
Trace pattern and cut box top and bottom from felt. Cut a 3½" strip for side piece. Starting at one corner, blanket stitch side strip to bottom piece and secure floss. Blanket stitch top piece in place leaving a 1½" opening at one end for stuffing. Cut off excess side strip and blanket stitch seam closed. Using funnel, pour rice into paperweight until it is half full. Stuff top half firmly with fiberfill. Blanket stitch opening closed. Glue embellishments as shown in photo.

Finish - Cut two ¾" strips of Red felt for ribbon. Wrap narrow strips around box, glue ends at top center. Cut a 1¼" x 8½" strip for bow. Cut a 1¼" x 8½" strip for bow tails, cut a vee in each end. Fold longer strip to form bow, center over tails, secure center with Red floss and glue in place. Cut tag from Tan felt. Write 'For You' with paint pen on tag and pin tag on top as shown in photo.

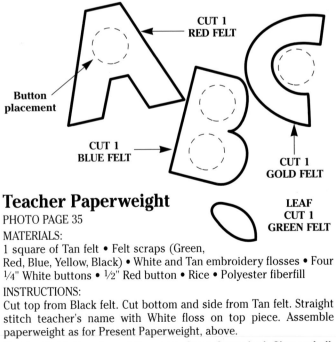

CUT 1
RED FELT

Button
placement

CUT 1
BLUE FELT

CUT 1
GOLD FELT

LEAF
CUT 1
GREEN FELT

Teacher Paperweight

PHOTO PAGE 35

MATERIALS:
1 square of Tan felt • Felt scraps (Green, Red, Blue, Yellow, Black) • White and Tan embroidery flosses • Four ¼" White buttons • ½" Red button • Rice • Polyester fiberfill

INSTRUCTIONS:
Cut top from Black felt. Cut bottom and side from Tan felt. Straight stitch teacher's name with White floss on top piece. Assemble paperweight as for Present Paperweight, above.

Finish - Cut letters from felt scraps. Cut a Green leaf. Glue embellishments as shown in photo.

Banner Dolls

Banner Dolls

GENERAL MATERIALS:

Muslin • Felt • Sewing threads • Embroidery flosses • Buttons • Two ½" and two ⅜" Black buttons • ¼" wood button plug • Mop yarn • 19 and 26 gauge wires • Black paint pen • Black acrylic paint • Small sponge brush • Cosmetic blush • Polyester fiberfill • Hot glue

ASSEMBLY INSTRUCTIONS:

Trace patterns and make templates.

Body - Transfer body patterns to muslin, cut out. Sew body, arms and legs using ¼" seams, leaving openings. Turn pieces to right side. Stuff body firmly. Hand stitch opening closed. Stuff arms and legs to within 1" of open ends. Gather stitch across ends, pull thread to close ends, secure thread. Sew arms and legs on body. Paint boots black, let dry. Sew ½" buttons on front of hands.

Jacket - Blanket stitch jacket pieces together with floss across shoul-

ders and along underarm seams, aligning raw edges. Cut center front of jacket. Blanket stitch around wrists, neckline, front openings and around hem.

Banner - Cut banner from felt. Write message on top piece with paint pen. Cut an 18" piece of 19 gauge wire. Blanket stitch banner pieces together with Red floss, holding wire across the center of banner back. Leave an opening at bottom of banner to stuff banner firmly with fiberfill, blanket stitch opening closed. Curl wire ends around paintbrush. Wrap wire ends around buttons on hands. Cut a 6" piece of 26 gauge wire to make hanger loop. Twist wire at center to form a loop and gently push ends through top center of banner back.

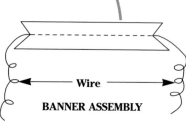

Wire

BANNER ASSEMBLY

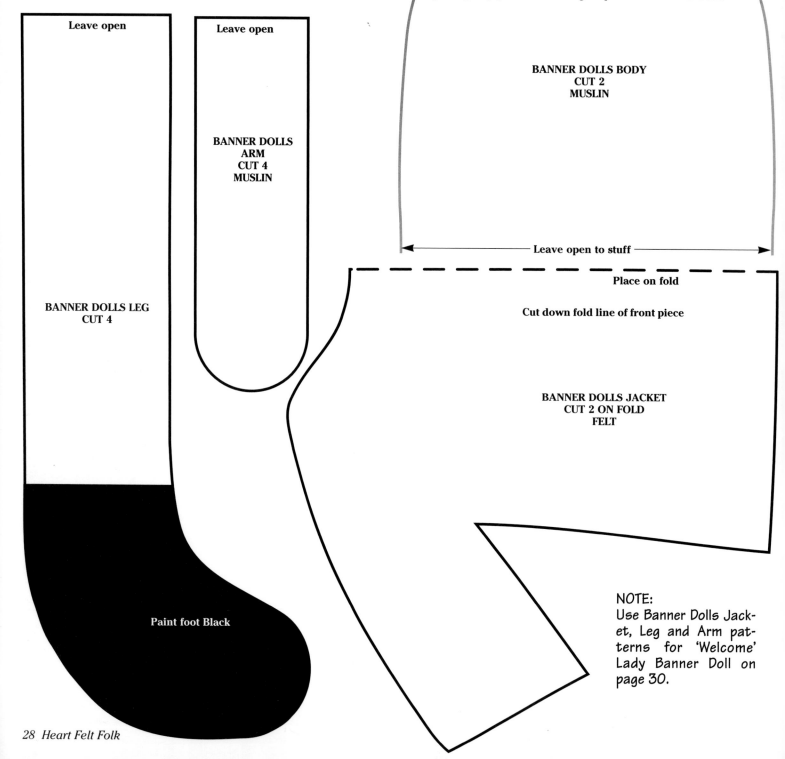

Leave open

Leave open

BANNER DOLLS ARM CUT 4 MUSLIN

BANNER DOLLS BODY CUT 2 MUSLIN

Leave open to stuff

BANNER DOLLS LEG CUT 4

Place on fold

Cut down fold line of front piece

BANNER DOLLS JACKET CUT 2 ON FOLD FELT

Paint foot Black

NOTE:
Use Banner Dolls Jacket, Leg and Arm patterns for 'Welcome' Lady Banner Doll on page 30.

Santa Claus Banner Doll

PHOTO PAGE 22

MATERIALS:

¼ yard of muslin • ½ yard of Red felt • 2 Antique Gold felt squares • Scrap of Navy Blue felt • White and Red sewing threads • White, Gold and Red embroidery flosses • Two ½" White buttons • Two ½" and two ³⁄₈" Black buttons • ¼" wood button plug • Mop yarn • Black paint pen

INSTRUCTIONS:

Body - Make body according to Assembly Instructions on page 28. Sew ½" buttons on fronts of hands.

Jacket - Cut jacket from Red felt and heart from Navy Blue felt. Assemble jacket with White floss blanket stitches. Straight stitch 'HO HO HO' on left jacket front with 2 strands of White floss. Blanket stitch heart on right jacket front with Gold floss. Sew ³⁄₈" buttons on right side of jacket center. Cut buttonholes in left side of jacket center to align with buttons. Place jacket on doll and button closed.

Pants - Cut pants from Red felt, stars from Gold felt. Use White floss to blanket stitch stars on knees of pants and sew White buttons in center of stars. Sew inside and outside seams of pants, turn to right side. Blanket stitch around bottom of legs with White floss. Sew running stitches around waist of pants, put pants on doll, pull thread tight around body and tie off. Tack pants in place in front and back.

Hat - Sew hat pieces together with a ¼" seam allowance. Glue 26 gauge wire into seam of hat. Turn right side out. Glue bell on tip of hat and hat on head. Shape hat. Twist 2 pieces of mop yarn together to form a cord, glue cord around bottom of hat.

Face - Draw eyes and eyebrows with pen. Rub blush on cheeks and across top of button plug nose. For beard, cut mop yarn into 3" and 4" pieces. Knot each piece in center and glue under cheeks and around back of head. Glue nose in place and glue one short knotted yarn piece under nose for mustache.

Banner - Cut banner from Gold felt. Write 'Merry Christmas!' on top piece with paint pen. Assemble banner according to Assembly Instructions on page 28.

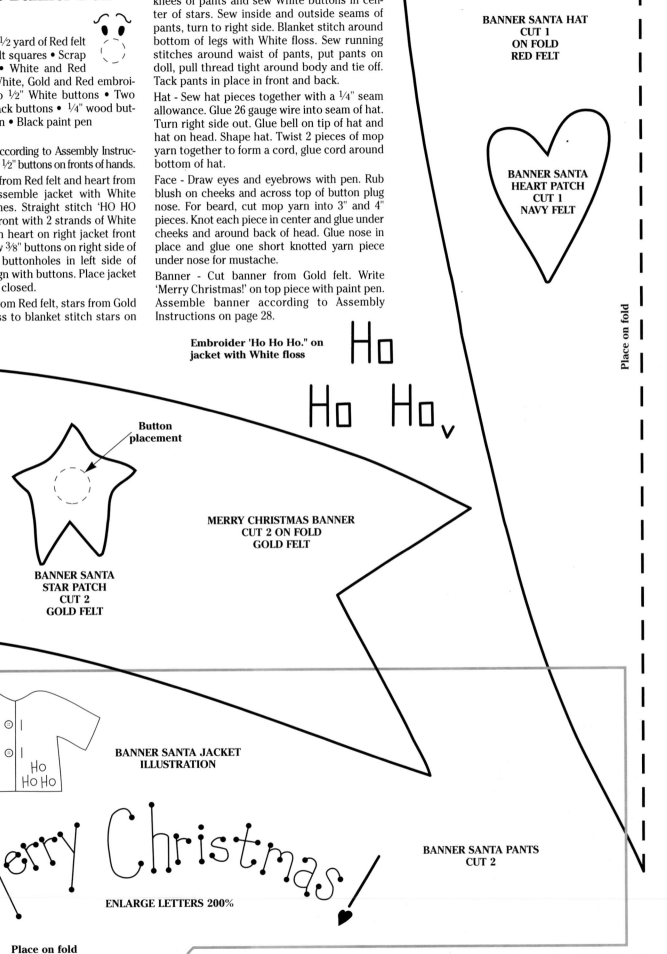

Embroider 'Ho Ho Ho." on jacket with White floss

Ho Ho Ho

Button placement

BANNER SANTA STAR PATCH CUT 2 GOLD FELT

MERRY CHRISTMAS BANNER CUT 2 ON FOLD GOLD FELT

BANNER SANTA HAT CUT 1 ON FOLD RED FELT

BANNER SANTA HEART PATCH CUT 1 NAVY FELT

Leave open

Place on fold

Place on fold

BANNER SANTA JACKET ILLUSTRATION

BANNER SANTA PANTS CUT 2

Merry Christmas!

ENLARGE LETTERS 200%

Waist - Place on fold

Place on fold

Another Banner Doll

'Welcome' Lady Banner Doll

PHOTO PAGE 34

MATERIALS:

¼ yard of muslin • ¼ yard of Green check fabric • 2 Blue felt squares • Tan felt square • Felt scraps (Persimmon, Green, Brown, Antique Gold) • White and Green sewing threads • White, Blue and Green embroidery flosses • 2 Pearl ¼" shank buttons • ¾" wood button • ½" buttons (1 Brown, 2 White, 5 Green) • 18" of ¾" Ecru lace • Small straw hat • Black and Red fine tip permanent markers

INSTRUCTIONS:

Trace patterns and make templates.

Body - Make body according to patterns and Assembly Instructions on page 28. Sew ½" White buttons on front of hands.

Dress - Cut dress from Green fabric. Sew side and shoulder seams, turn to right side. Place dress on doll. Sew running stitches ¼" from ends of sleeves with Green floss, pull tight and tack in place. Tack neck edge in place if necessary. Glue 6" of lace around neck and wood button on lace, cut off excess lace. Make running stitches ¾" from bottom of dress, gather loosely and tie off.

Jacket - (See pattern on page 28.) Cut jacket from Blue felt. Assemble jacket with Blue floss blanket stitches. Blanket stitch around wrists with Blue floss. Cut center front of jacket. Blanket stitch neckline, front openings and around hem with Green floss. Fold down corners at neckline, tack with Blue floss. For flower, cut Gold star and Brown center. Cut a Green leaf and a Green ¼" x 2" stem. Cut Persimmon pumpkin, cut a Green ⅛" x 2½" vine and Green stem. Draw lines on pumpkin with paint pen. Glue pumpkin, leaf, tendril and Blue button on right side of jacket front. Glue star, center, Brown button, stem and leaf on left side. Sew Pearl buttons on jacket as shown in photo. Place jacket on doll. Tie buttons together with White floss, if desired.

Boots - Glue 6" of lace around top of each boot, cut off excess. Tie White floss through 2 Green buttons, glue on lace.

Face - Draw eyes, nose, eyebrows and eyelashes with Black marker and mouth with Red marker. Rub blush on cheeks. For hair, wrap curly yarn around fingers in a figure 8. Tie strands in center and glue on top of head. Cut ends of loops and shape hair as desired. Glue hat on head.

Banner - Cut banner from Tan felt. Write 'Welcome!' on top piece with paint pen. Assemble banner according to Assembly

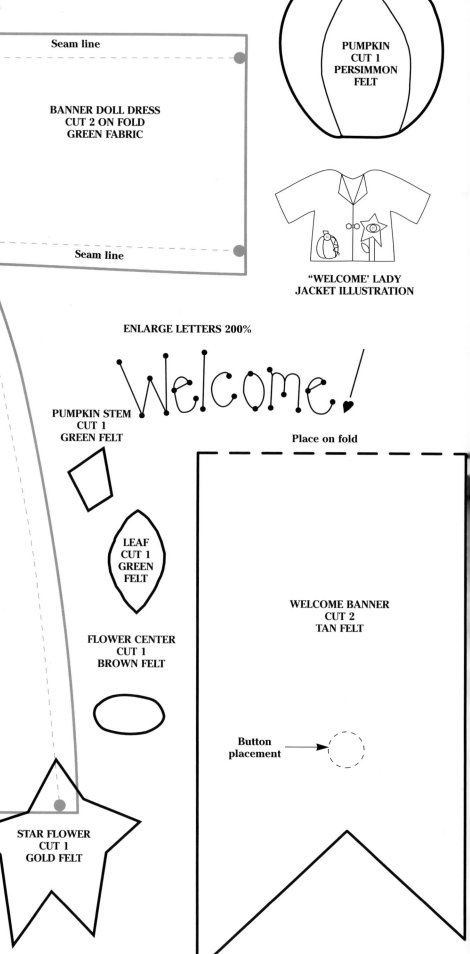

PUMPKIN
CUT 1
PERSIMMON
FELT

BANNER DOLL DRESS
CUT 2 ON FOLD
GREEN FABRIC

Seam line

Seam line

"WELCOME' LADY
JACKET ILLUSTRATION

ENLARGE LETTERS 200%

Welcome!

PUMPKIN STEM
CUT 1
GREEN FELT

Place on fold

LEAF
CUT 1
GREEN
FELT

FLOWER CENTER
CUT 1
BROWN FELT

WELCOME BANNER
CUT 2
TAN FELT

Button
placement

STAR FLOWER
CUT 1
GOLD FELT

Place on fold

Heart Felt Nativity Dolls
Celebrate the Season.

Book Covers

Friendship Book Cover

PHOTO PAGE 35

MATERIALS:

Used hardback book • Tan felt • Felt scraps (Red, Yellow, Blue, Green, Ivory) • 4 Pearl ³⁄₈" buttons • Four ¹⁄₂" buttons • Black paint pen

INSTRUCTIONS:

Cut Tan felt to cover front of book, glue edges in place. Trace patterns and cut 4 backgrounds from Ivory and 4 hearts from remaining felt colors. Glue backgrounds and hearts in place. Write 'Your friendship warms my heart' with paint pen as shown in photo. Glue buttons on hearts as shown in photo.

BACKGROUND CUT 4 IVORY

HEART CUT 1 EACH GREEN BLUE RED YELLOW

Teacher Book Cover

PHOTO PAGE 35

MATERIALS:

Used hardback book • Black felt • 1" torn strips of Red/Black check fabric • ¹⁄₂" strips of Gold print fabric • White paint pen • Four assorted ¹⁄₂" buttons

INSTRUCTIONS:

Cut Black felt to cover front of book, glue edges in place. Glue Red fabric strips around edges of felt, overlapping corners. Glue Gold strips inside Red strips, overlapping corners. Draw designs and write letters and numbers with pen. Glue buttons in place at corners of Gold strips.

Sunflower Pin

PHOTO PAGE 34

MATERIALS:
Scraps of Kelly Green and Antique Gold felt • Scrap of Brown check fabric • 1/2" Brown button • Green and Gold embroidery flosses • Polyester fiberfill • Hot glue

INSTRUCTIONS:
Trace and transfer patterns to felt, cut out. Blanket stitch sunflower pieces together, leaving an opening along one long side of a petal. Stuff lightly with fiberfill, blanket stitch opening closed. Repeat to assemble stem. Glue stem on back of sunflower. Cut circle of check fabric for yo yo. Fold edge of circle down 1/8", sew running stitches around edge, pull stitches tight and tie off. Sew yo yo on center of flower through all layers. Glue button on yo yo center.

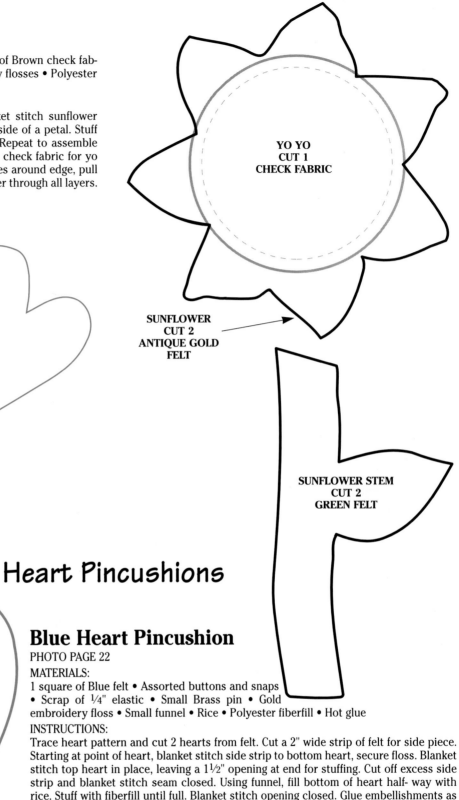

YO YO
CUT 1
CHECK FABRIC

SUNFLOWER
CUT 2
ANTIQUE GOLD
FELT

SUNFLOWER STEM
CUT 2
GREEN FELT

Heart Pincushions

HEART
CUT 1

Blue Heart Pincushion

PHOTO PAGE 22

MATERIALS:
1 square of Blue felt • Assorted buttons and snaps • Scrap of 1/4" elastic • Small Brass pin • Gold embroidery floss • Small funnel • Rice • Polyester fiberfill • Hot glue

INSTRUCTIONS:
Trace heart pattern and cut 2 hearts from felt. Cut a 2" wide strip of felt for side piece. Starting at point of heart, blanket stitch side strip to bottom heart, secure floss. Blanket stitch top heart in place, leaving a 1 1/2" opening at end for stuffing. Cut off excess side strip and blanket stitch seam closed. Using funnel, fill bottom of heart half- way with rice. Stuff with fiberfill until full. Blanket stitch opening closed. Glue embellishments as shown in photo.

Pink Heart Pincushion

PHOTO PAGE 35

MATERIALS:
1 square of Pink felt • 12" of 1 1/2" Cream wire edge grosgrain ribbon • Assorted buttons and snaps • Cream embroidery floss • Small funnel • Rice • Polyester fiberfill • Hot glue

INSTRUCTIONS:
Assemble as for Blue Heart Pincushion, above.